# ESSENTIAL
## MANAGERS

# LEADERSHIP

W9-COJ-539

# ESSENTIAL
## MANAGERS

# LEADERSHIP

**Produced for DK by Dynamo Ltd**
1 Cathedral Court, Southernhay East, Exeter, EX1 1AF

**Written by Christina Osborne**

**Senior Art Editor** Helen Spencer
**Senior Editor** Chauney Dunford
**US Editor** Karyn Gerhard
**Jacket Design Development Manager** Sophia MTT
**Jacket Designers** Akiko Kato, Juhi Sheth
**Producer** Nancy-Jane Maun
**Production Editor** Gillian Reid
**Senior Managing Art Editor** Lee Griffiths
**Managing Editor** Gareth Jones
**Associate Publishing Director** Liz Wheeler
**Art Director** Karen Self
**Design Director** Philip Ormerod
**Publishing Director** Jonathan Metcalf

This American Edition, 2021
First American Edition, 2008
Published in the United States by DK Publishing
1450 Broadway, Suite 801, New York, NY 10018

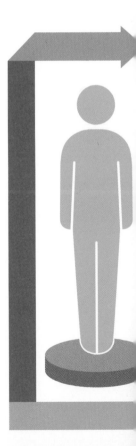

A catalog record for this book is available from the Library of Congress.
ISBN 978-0-7440-3506-3

DK books are available at special discounts when purchased in bulk for
sales promotions, premiums, fund-raising, or educational use. For details,
contact: DK Publishing Special Markets, 1450 Broadway, Suite 801,
New York, NY 10018 or SpecialSales@dk.com

Printed and bound in China

## For the curious
www.dk.com

# Contents

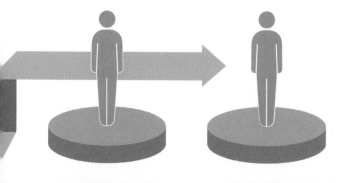

# Introduction

**Leadership** is the ability to create an environment where everyone knows what contribution is expected and feels totally committed to doing a great job. Leadership is an essential skill for all successful managers to learn and practice regularly.

This book explains the key techniques leaders use to release their own and their team's full potential. It shows you how to think and take action with a leadership approach and to look at yourself and the world around you with a leadership focus.

Practical advice is given to help you to develop the leadership aspects of your own role and to encourage leadership and initiative from everyone in your team, including those working remotely. From taking up a leadership role to leading with confidence in difficult situations and motivating staff both in person and from a distance, this book prepares you step-by-step for all the challenges leaders face.

The book is packed with advice to help you direct your energy toward building essential relationships and achieving the most important results that add value to your organization and identify you as a successful leader of people.

# Understanding
## **leadership**

When you take up a leadership role, you will be expected
to juggle multiple tasks—from meeting goals to developing
new business opportunities—with multiple responsibilities.
In today's fast-changing world, that means not only making
sure your team follows the same organizational vision and
values, but also managing risk and building resilience.

01

# Defining the challenge

**If you thrive on thinking creatively, inspiring and guiding people, experimenting with different approaches, and making intuitive decisions, you are on the way to being a leader. But truly accomplished leaders also possess sound problem-solving skills, a strong vision, and empathy.**

## Thinking leadership

Leaders are made rather than born. And while a real desire to lead is a prerequisite for leadership, the key skills you need to lead can be learned. Leadership has many facets: it is the ability to inspire others to overcome challenges, accept continuous change, and achieve goals. It is the capacity to build strong, effective teams, and use your influence to persuade and steer. It is about having a vision and values, and about taking care of the people around you. The old idea of one person at the top issuing orders is on its way out. Leadership now is about creating the conditions for all to rise, and building the structures and cultures that empower any team member to lead when required. In today's dynamic world, we are all potential leaders.

**MANAGEMENT**

**Tip**

**BE NIMBLE**
To be a **good leader,** stay close to your team, and use your **judgment** to move between leadership and management roles as necessary.

## BEING A LEADER

| Dos | Don'ts |
|-----|--------|
| O **Learning quickly what motivates team members** | O Thinking yesterday's result will still count tomorrow |
| O **Asking your team for their views on the situation** | O Being out of touch with your own emotions |
| O **Thinking beyond what happens in the short term** | O Not noticing what is going on around you |
| O **Knowing how to train and develop your team** | O Not asking for feedback on your leadership and ideas |
| O **Setting standards to build a team you can rely on** | O Not keeping physically fit and thinking positively |

**LEADERSHIP**

A **leader** creates a bold vision and **inspires others** to believe in it, while a **manager** puts the vision into practice by **steering the actions of staff**

## Leading and managing

Leadership is a substantially different role from management. A leader is someone who creates a bold vision and inspires others to believe in it, while a manager seeks to put the vision into practice by steering the day-to-day actions and behaviors of her or his employees. You probably aspire to be called a leader rather than a manager but, despite their differences, the two roles remain intrinsically linked. Sound management requires some leadership skills, and great leaders are—or know what it takes to be—good managers.

When you move into a leadership role you won't and can't abandon managing altogether. To be credible as a leader, you need to acknowledge the past and what is currently happening, at the same time as focusing on the future.

# Leading from within

**The job of a leader is to give others a sense of purpose and self-worth. This is impossible to do with any conviction if you don't understand your own strengths and weaknesses, or if you are uncertain about the direction in which you want to take your professional and personal life. Improving self-awareness is an essential part of growing into a more effective leader and becoming alert to the effects you are having on others.**

## Being a frontrunner

People respect leaders who embrace strong values and take responsibility for their own choices in life. To demonstrate this internal strength you need to be seen to be leading by example. Show your team that you have the confidence to take risks, that you can persist through difficult times, and that you are prepared to keep on learning, adapting, and creating new business opportunities, as well as listening to their needs.

## Defining thinking styles

| STYLE | CHARACTERISTICS | QUESTIONS ASKED |
|---|---|---|
| TACTICAL | O Accepts direction<br>O Focuses on how to achieve **a goal**<br>O **Plans** and thinks through any actions **logically** | O How can we achieve the best result in the least time?<br>O How can we organize the actions into a clear plan?<br>O What are the most important things to do or coordinate? |
| OPERATIONAL | O Sees **opportunities** for action and improvement<br>O Focuses on **practical actions** and implementation in complex situations | O What action can we take?<br>O What needs to be done?<br>O When can we start? |
| STRATEGIC | O Thinks out any problems from **first principles**<br>O Redefines problems and **confidently** challenges issues upward | O What if...?<br>O Why have we ruled out these other courses of action?<br>O Why not do this instead?<br>O Who else needs to be involved? |

## Knowing yourself

People don't all think in the same way. Understanding your own thinking style and the styles of others around you will give you some valuable leadership tools. The term "thinking style" does not refer to your IQ, but how you process information. Broadly, we can distinguish between three styles: tactical, operational, and strategic.

Most people tend to get stuck using just one of the thinking styles. But by recognizing your own thinking style you begin to ask different questions and think about problems in fresh and exciting new ways. By doing this you work more effectively with your team because you can understand how they think and communicate, and you can talk to people in their own "language."

**Tip**

### LIST YOUR SKILLS

Make a list of the essential characteristics you already have as a leader—**"I am focused," "I am committed to excellence," "I respect others," "I work hard"**—and those to which you aspire: **"I am caring," "I am trusted."** Repeat this exercise regularly to monitor your inner thoughts and development.

We can recognize three **thinking styles:** tactical, operational, and strategic

## Leadership styles

Psychologist Daniel Goleman popularized the concept of Emotional Intelligence (see pp.16–17). He developed the idea that emotions are important in management, and identified six leadership styles (see below). Many people use several styles at different times. Goleman found that the visionary style had the most positive impact, but coaching is increasingly key.

> When you **embrace the values** by which you live and apply them to your **role as a leader**, people will respect your **sincerity** and sense that you **wish others to succeed**

**Leadership styles**

### COMMANDING

- O Demands that people comply
- O Drive to achieve, self-control
- O **Key phrase:** "Do what I tell you"
- O Negative impact

### VISIONARY

- O Leads with a clear vision
- O Self-confidence, empathy
- O **Key phrase:** "Come with me"
- O Most positive impact

### AFFILIATIVE

- O Creates harmony, builds bonds
- O Empathy, good relationships, and communication skills
- O **Key phrase:** "People come first"
- O Positive impact

## Developing self-awareness

To be effective, you need to lead from the inside out—what you really think and value should emerge in your behavior. To think as a leader, you should look to your self-awareness as well as your awareness of the outside world.

Leading from within is not just about being true to your own principles—it also brings results. When you embrace the values by which you live and apply them to your role as a leader, people will respect your sincerity, acknowledge the stake you have in your work and in your team, and sense that you wish others to succeed. Growing self-awareness means analyzing your thoughts and emotions, seeking as much feedback from others as possible, and developing keen listening skills.

### DEMOCRATIC

O Consensus through participation

O Collaboration, team spirit, and communication skills

O **Key phrase:** "What do you think?"

O Positive impact

### PACESETTING

O Sets high performance standards

O Drive to achieve, conscientiousness

O **Key phrase:** "Do as I do"

O Negative impact

### COACHING

O Develops skills in other people

O Developing others, empathy, self-awareness

O **Key phrase:** "Try this"

O Positive impact

O Now increasingly important

**Tip**

**COMMIT TO CHANGE**
Seek out an **experienced** coach to guide you in building **EI.** The **transformation** means you changing your **attitudes** and habits, as well as learning **new skills,** and requires a real **commitment**—in time and resources—from you and from your organization.

## Applying self-knowledge

The benefits of self-knowledge in the workplace may not be immediately apparent when set alongside other, more practical and cognitive skills, but its value has been acknowledged by psychologists for decades. The term Emotional Intelligence (EI) was coined to describe an ability to identify, discriminate between, and use one's own and others' feelings to guide your thoughts and actions. The importance of EI cannot be overstated—there are many studies that indicate that EI is a much better indicator of leadership potential than standard measures of intelligence such as IQ. The emotions that leaders experience affect the culture of an organization, shaping productivity, employee satisfaction, and loyalty, and having a real influence on results.

**Using emotional intelligence**

RECOGNIZING EMOTIONS

REGULATING EMOTIONS

USING EMOTIONS

EMPATHIZING

NURTURING

The **emotions** that **leaders experience** affect the **culture** of an organization

## Assessing the benefits

Understanding and controlling your inner self has some real applications that benefit you and the organization:

- Being able to control your temper, to elevate yourself from boredom, or to turn dejection into positive energy are all desirable abilities.

- Knowing that sad or negative moods tend to bring your focus to details, while happy moods direct you to new ideas and solutions, improves your productivity and time management.

- Confronting and analyzing your fears may illuminate a problem you are facing, so this may lead to a solution and save you time.

Expertise in the key competencies of Emotional Intelligence opens the door to more sophisticated ways of forming and sustaining productive relationships (see pp.34–37). What's more, these competencies can be learned through training and practice. So you will be able to change your behavior in a genuine, sustained manner.

---

O Accurately **identifying and categorizing** your own feelings and the feelings of others.

O **Being aware,** moment-by-moment, of what you are feeling.

---

O Recognizing that **how you feel influences how you think.**

O Knowing **which of your moods** are best for different situations.

O Not letting others **manipulate** your emotions.

---

O Using **deliberate strategies** to make your feelings—even negative ones—work for you.

O Harnessing emotions so that you can take **positive actions,** even in the face of difficulty.

---

O Recognizing that **emotions provide information** about others.

O Being able to **see a situation** from another's point-of-view.

---

O Genuinely **caring** for others.

O Showing **real appreciation** for peoples' contributions.

O Having others' best interests at heart when setting goals.

# Leading through vision

**As a business leader, you will be expected to set out the values of an organization and provide its stakeholders with an emotionally appealing and achievable vision of the future. You will need clear, thoughtful communication at every level in order to develop this vision and translate it into medium-term strategies and day-to-day action.**

## Setting out the vision

Leaders focus on developing a vision and overall aims, and inspiring and helping team members as they figure out how to achieve the agreed objectives in a way consistent with the organization's values.

A business vision is a description of your future as a team or organization. It outlines what things will look like when we get to where we want to be. Your leadership role may be to develop the vision and strategic objectives at the top of your organization, or it may be to devise your team plan in alignment with a bigger corporate strategy.

**Tip**

### EXPLAIN WHY

"Why" needs to be **explained** in two ways: "Because of A..." (referring to a past/present reason) and "In order to do B..." (explaining possible **future consequences).**

## Developing the vision

Involve your team in developing the vision from the start—if they are shaping it early on, they will be more likely to embrace it. Begin by writing it down. As you move forward, you will need to restate and recreate the vision by communicating with your team through open question-and-answer sessions, one-on-one reviews, and team meetings. Soon each person will learn how to make a meaningful individual contribution toward team goals.

People are motivated by a clear understanding of what they need to do to fulfill the vision, by when, how well, and why. These are key signposts on the journey to their professional development and to the achievement of the team's vision. Your job is to help everyone in your team to plan the route, and to review their progress.

**In focus**

### JUST REWARDS

Think laterally about the way you reward members of your team. Financial rewards often have less motivational value than your recognition and thanks. If you are respected by your team, your greatest gift is your time. Make time to give full attention to each person in your team at regular intervals. Never over-promise and under-deliver future benefits to your team members.

Each person will learn how to make **a contribution** toward **team goals**

## **Working with teams**

Your key tasks as leader are to inspire emotional attachment to the vision developed and to make success visible. This will help team members see that their individual work counts and that doing their best really does lead to a better life for all concerned.

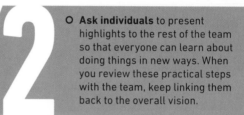

O **Give everyone a role** to play in implementing the team vision and ask them to report back to you on what has gone exceptionally well and what has gone not so well.

O **Ask individuals** to present highlights to the rest of the team so that everyone can learn about doing things in new ways. When you review these practical steps with the team, keep linking them back to the overall vision.

O **Remember to say** "thank you" individually and in front of the team to help them keep their momentum and motivation.

O **Celebrate team successes** to keep the team moving forward together. Recognize even small steps in the right direction.

O **Explore** with individual team members their unique mix of values, life experiences, knowledge, and skills, plus potential abilities. Understand what specifically motivates each person to engage with their work and willingly release the extra they have to give.

# Growing with your role

**Growth is built into the vision of most organizations; and when an organization grows, its leaders must be prepared to adapt with it. Your role as a leader may become bigger and more strategic with each organizational transition, so anticipating change is a cornerstone of thinking like an effective leader.**

## Start-up

When an organization starts up, it is entrepreneurial—focused on delivering a new service to new customers. Often, communication is informal, and people are prepared to put in long hours. Customer feedback is quick and the small group of people responds rapidly with enthusiasm and energy.

Leadership at this stage is about keeping close to customers and staff, and encouraging new ideas. As a leader, you may well be involved in frontline activities as well as decisions.

# 3x

**more revenue**
is generated by
**founder-run** large
US companies
over 15 years

## Rapid growth

As the organization grows, you may start to see problems with the quality of delivery. Communication with the team may become more formal and some of the initial energy and initiative can be lost. More of your time will be spent on designing and implementing systems, structures, and standards.

At this stage, you need to work hard at remaining accessible to people who seek your advice and resist retreating into a purely management role.

## Continued growth

The next organizational transition occurs when you begin to realize that you can no longer control everything—there are not enough hours in the day. You may notice that team members are complaining about how long it takes for decisions to be made. They may ask for greater freedom to make their own decisions.

At this point, you should begin to recognize the need to delegate— essential if you are to retain and develop staff. You should be putting increasing amounts of your time and effort into leadership and communication and less into your original expertise— for example, accounting, sales, marketing, engineering, or operations.

> You should be putting **increasing amounts** of your time and effort into **leadership and communication**

## Devolution

As the organization continues to grow, you may become part of a high-level core leadership team directing strategy and coordination, while a group of managers in business units lead teams on a devolved basis.

You need to become a strong communicator, because a significant part of your role is resolving tensions between devolved units and the center. You need to manage relationships to ensure that all parts of the organization work collaboratively and are fully committed to the overall strategy. Bear in mind the development of future leaders is essential to the long-term survival of the organization and is another one of your new responsibilities.

# Taking up your
# **leadership role**

When you are given a leadership position, you need to
prepare yourself for intense learning and adaptation.
Whether you're a new recruit or moving up internally,
there are many challenges in store, from learning the
lay of the land to developing your competences.

02

# Preparing to lead

**When you become a leader, you need to quickly understand what is expected from you and from your team. Your employer will provide you with guidance, but don't assume that you'll get the complete picture. A lot of the groundwork is going to be up to you.**

### Giving yourself a head start

It pays to prepare for your leadership role even before your first day on the job. Do some basic groundwork and research: ask your employer where you fit into their organizational plans; ask when you will be expected to produce objectives for your team; and when and how your performance—and that of your team—will be assessed. If possible, ask to meet the outgoing leader and discuss the demands of the role and the team dynamics. Research your team: request performance figures and personnel files; ask the outgoing leader and your peers what information will be of most use.

**Ask your employer** where you fit into their **organizational plans**

### Managing data

Throughout the first few weeks in your new role, you will be deluged with information. Unfortunately, you won't necessarily know which of this data is of strategic importance, and which is just minor detail. Head off early errors by being systematic; file the information and make a list of everything you have received. Review this list weekly and try to place the relative significance of each piece of information in a broader context.

**23%**
**increase** in performance may result from **best management practice**

## Managing people

You'll also be introduced to many new people throughout the organization. After each meeting, make a note of the name, position, and distinguishing features of the person you have met, along with anything memorable they said to you. When you meet them next, you'll remember who they are and how they fit into the organization; moreover, you'll be able to pick up your conversation with them.

## CHECKLIST...
Exchanging information

| | YES | NO |
|---|---|---|
| **1** Have you had or requested an **induction briefing**? | ☐ | ☐ |
| **2** Have you **identified** areas in your **new role** where you need training? | ☐ | ☐ |
| **3** Have you studied the company's **organization charts**? | ☐ | ☐ |
| **4** If you have been **promoted**, have you told your existing **contacts** in the organization of your new role? | ☐ | ☐ |
| **5** Do you know which **meetings** you are expected to attend? | ☐ | ☐ |

**Tip**

**ASK FOR SUPPORT**
If you have been **promoted internally**, people will assume you have a good knowledge of your organization. But you will still need **support** in transferring to your new role—so don't be afraid to **ask for it**.

02
01

## Being realistic

Your arrival as a team's new leader will raise expectations of change for the better. However, you may discover that some expectations are less than realistic. For example, your team's previous leader may have provided detailed guidance on how work should be carried out. If your leadership style is more about empowering your team to make their own decisions, they may initially feel poorly supported and even resentful of the added responsibility. Early in your tenure, ask others what assumptions they have about you and your role.

- Outline what success looks like to you. Does their view match yours?
- What expectations do they have of how long things will take?
- Have they been made any unrealistic promises about what you will deliver?

You can then begin to address any discrepancies between their expectations and your reality.

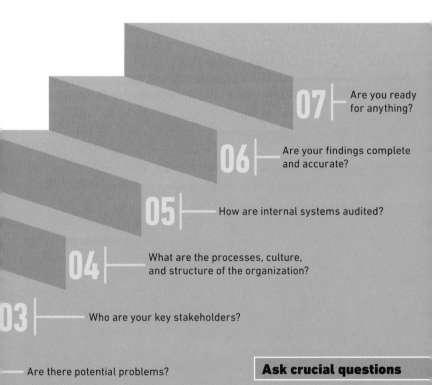

**07** — Are you ready for anything?

**06** — Are your findings complete and accurate?

**05** — How are internal systems audited?

**04** — What are the processes, culture, and structure of the organization?

**03** — Who are your key stakeholders?

— Are there potential problems?

**Ask crucial questions**

What are the aims of your organization or team?

# Focusing your energy

**As a leader, you are likely to be inundated with communications, requests, new tasks, and initiatives. Recognizing—and focusing on—what is really important is critical to your success and that of your team; it is vital that how you spend your time reflects your priorities.**

## How to prioritize tasks

### HIGH URGENCY: LOW IMPORTANCE

**Typical activities**

O Dealing with messages as they come in

O Dealing with others' priorities not in line with your vision

**What happens when you spend time on this**

O Lack of clear goals

O Crisis management

O Feeling out of control

O Behaving inconsistently

**Action: Delegate it**

### LOW URGENCY: LOW IMPORTANCE

**Typical activities**

O Low-level meetings

O Time-wasting

O Unfocused browsing

**What happens when you spend time on this**

O Failure to take responsibility

O Inability to complete jobs

O Increased dependence on others

O Insecurity

**Action: Leave it**

URGENCY — HIGH / LOW

LOW          IMPORTANCE

## Managing your time

It is easy to get distracted from key tasks by less important, but nonetheless urgent, activities. Prioritizing your actions is something you should schedule in every day, and approach with discipline. A simple solution is to write a "to do" list at the end of each day. Scrutinize this list, assessing each item against your vision, values, and key objectives; then, number each item in order of priority. Alternatively, try categorizing your tasks more systematically under the four headings shown below.

### HIGH URGENCY: HIGH IMPORTANCE

**Typical activities**

O Dealing with crises

O Being closely involved with time-critical projects

O Attending key meetings

**What happens when you spend time on this**

O Constant crisis management

O Exhaustion and stress

O Burnout over the long-term

**Action: Do it now, but review your time planning**

### LOW URGENCY: HIGH IMPORTANCE

**Typical activities**

O Planning ahead

O Anticipating problems

O Guiding and training the team

O Delegating

O Building relationships

**What happens when you spend time on this**

O Overview

O Vision

O Balance

**Action: Schedule it**

**IMPORTANCE**      **HIGH**

## WORKING SMART

| Dos | Don'ts |
|---|---|
| O **Improving standards** | O Doing work you could delegate |
| O **Building networks** | O Never leaving your work space |
| O **Recording and analyzing how you spend your time** | O Reacting to stimuli as they arrive |
| O **Being realistic about durations** | O Starting without a clear schedule |

### Getting back on track

Missed or delayed deadlines and recurring problems that you never seem to get around to fixing are symptoms of faulty time management. If the root cause is not addressed, your work life could soon run out of control, sapping your energy and stifling your creativity. Stop, take some time out, and refocus your thoughts. Plan in some time to address strategic activities, and think what you could do to improve delegation within your team.

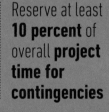

Reserve at least **10 percent** of overall **project time for contingencies**

### Tip

**MAKE ROOM FOR CONTINGENCIES**

You should set aside time with your team to **brainstorm** likely barriers to delivering on time. **Reserve** at least **10 percent** of overall project time for **contingencies.**

## Delegating successfully

Delegation is a critical leadership skill, and one that—when done well—has great benefits for you and your team. It liberates your schedule, makes members of your team feel valued, and develops capabilities in people throughout the organization. Delegating well requires more than just handing a task over to a subordinate; there are many issues you need to consider carefully before you act.

### How to delegate

O Choose carefully **to whom you delegate a task.** Assess the probability of things going wrong.

O Only delegate tasks that can be **clearly defined.** If you can't specify the desired outcome and timeframe, it is unreasonable to expect someone to succeed.

O Delegate **time-consuming, recurring** tasks.

O Establish and agree on **milestones,** working procedures, resources, and **deadlines.**

O Check that the person to whom you are delegating **shares your understanding** of the task in hand.

O Monitor progress and provide support, but avoid micromanaging. **You cannot abdicate responsibility,** but if you delegate well, you can trust people to do a good job.

O Delegating means allowing people to **find their own solutions:** you must accept that these will not necessarily be the same as your solutions.

O Don't apportion blame if things don't work out: remember it is you who **shoulders responsibility** for ultimate success or failure.

## Selecting personnel

To identify the best member of your team to take on a particular task, try using a "Plan to Delegate" table, such as the sample at right, to give a degree of objectivity when making a decision. To use the Plan to Delegate table:

- List all members of your team.
- Devise your criteria for choosing someone—those on the sample table are a good starting point.
- Rate each member of your team for all criteria from 1–10.
- Add the scores.
- Add comments on the type of training, development, or support each individual needs. Do they need short-term input, intensive support, or long-term guidance?

With this exercise, you will see that the best candidate is not always the most obvious. You may have developed the habit of just asking one experienced and skilled team member to do jobs for you. However, others on the team may have more time to devote to the task, and will benefit from the experience and responsibility.

**1/3** more **revenue** is generated by US CEOs who are top **delegators**

### Tip

**SCHEDULE A DEBRIEF**
Once a task is **complete,** **allow time** for a debrief—discuss what went well, and what did not. How would you **change the process** next time? What was **learned?** Was this a **suitable** task to delegate to the individual?

### Plan to delegate

**CRITERIA**

Current capability and experience

Skills/competences

Development potential

Availability

Motivation/commitment

Task consistent with individual's goals for development

**Total score**

Other comments, such as training or support needed

**Milestones/reviews**

| JAMAL | JIM | JANE |
|-------|-----|------|
| 8 | 7 | 4 |
| 7 | 8 | 5 |
| 9 | 7 | 9 |
| 3 | 9 | 9 |
| 8 | 4 | 9 |
| 5 | 3 | 7 |
| **40** | **38** | **43** |
| None | Needs constant motivation | Needs training on template usage |
| **Review at end of task** | **Review frequently** | **Review at first milestone and end only** |

# Working at relationships

**From your earliest days as a leader, you will need to build relationships with your team and a range of stakeholders throughout the organization. The ability to understand and empathize with people is a key skill, and thinking of relationships in terms of "stories" gives you tools to understand what drives others and help productive interpersonal relationships thrive.**

## Telling stories

We each carry in our heads our own stories—the narratives we have constructed over the years to make sense of our collected experiences, emotions, habits, and thoughts. These stories bias our perspective in all new situations and may push us toward embracing challenges or, conversely, constrain our actions.

Relationships are built by exchanging these stories with other people we meet. As we tell our stories, we disclose more about ourselves, our backgrounds, roles, and beliefs—and create new, emergent stories. Just as individuals have their own stories, so do organizations; these stories encompass the history and values of that organization and describe how they get things done.

# 85%

of CEOs **agree** a firm's financial performance is tied to **empathy**

Do the stories **convey a strong moral code,** judgments, or beliefs?

## Listening to stories

By listening empathetically to a person's story, you may be able to understand why they want to work with you and their likely motivations. It's about grasping what the other person is experiencing from their frame of reference, not yours. Stories also point to ways of negotiating with individuals or organizations, and even indicate if a joint venture will succeed. Leaders who fail to take account of a person's or firm's past thoughts, culture, actions, and aspirations—as well as what they observe in the present—may face an unexpected culture clash. A lack of empathy and sensitivity gets in the way of team performance, innovation, learning, and business success.

**Tip**

### LISTEN TO THE SUBTEXT
**Listen** for recurrent patterns in **people's stories.** What do they **tell you** about the way they **relate** to others, their modes of thinking, biases, and barriers?

Do the stories **express** themselves in **protective** jargon?

Do the stories claim particular **skills** for the individual?

Are the stories **explorative** and **adventurous,** or conservative, **focused** on maintaining equilibrium?

Do the stories place the individual in a **particular role**—hero, participant, or victim, for example?

Are the stories mostly set in the **past, present, or future?**

Do the stories make or break **connections** between things?

## Case study

### BOOSTING THE BOTTOM LINE

When Riikka Mattila joined Scandic Hotels in 2012 as its HR director for Finalnd, employee engagement was the lowest of all six countries in which the group operated. Taking an empathetic approach, Riikka focused on bolstering leadership, forging trust, and empowering staff. Each employee was asked to give input on how they did their jobs on the group's online learning platform.

Initially, participation was low, so the firm asked employees what changes might make them use it. Persistence paid off and at the Great Place to Work awards in 2018, Scandic Hotels won best workplace in Finland for the second year running, and third best workplace in Europe. The return on investment was lower employee turnover, improved financial performance, and more satisfied customers.

## Learning from stories

By listening empathetically to the stories people tell, you gain an insight into what drives them and how they relate to others. This doesn't just build better working relationships, it also gives you a competitive advantage. Empathy filters through into increased customer satisfaction, happier employees, higher revenue, and a stronger brand. Be aware that it takes extra effort to forge relationships with people you don't meet in person. Building trust when you can't pick up on the visual cues we all use when talking requires you to listen more carefully, communicate more clearly, and be even more open and flexible.

Psychologists Daniel Goleman and Paul Ekman identify three facets of empathy:

- **Cognitive empathy** helps in understanding how a person feels and what they are thinking.
- **Emotional empathy** aids identification with another's feelings and deepens relationships.
- **Empathic concern** provides motivation to help others.

Empathy is a skill that can be developed, especially if you practice it every day. Park your ego and focus on how your work benefits others; in meetings, ensure you know what would fulfil your colleagues' goals rather than only focusing on what you want. You can then achieve the kind of win-win solutions that keep employees engaged.

> Park your **ego** and focus on how your work **benefits others**

Seeing something from another's perspective is key. Empathy doesn't mean getting in the other person's head to manipulate them, but knowing how best to work together. If you feel someone is "being difficult," reframe it by reflecting on their story. People don't usually set out to be difficult, but may have a driver that you don't understand. With empathy, you can find out what it is.

## Supporting collaboration

Empathetic leadership creates workplaces that, in the words of Harvard Business School professor Amy Edmondson, are "psychologically safe." Her work has shown that organizations with higher psychological safety perform better on almost every metric, from innovation to revenue. The term covers four main areas:

- **Willingness to help** Encouraging people to collaborate, explore better solutions, and build new narratives, so everyone wins.

- **Openness** Making it safe for people to speak up with ideas or questions, without being ignored or put down.
- **Risk/failure** Viewing mistakes as a chance to learn, so people continue to express their ideas, nudge their comfort zones, and take on challenges.
- **Inclusivity** Allowing people to be their authentic selves and valuing them for it.

Psychological safety is not about creating an "anything goes" environment. It's about minimizing anxiety and using empathy and respect, not fear, to motivate.

## How psychologically safe is your organization?

**PSYCHOLOGICAL SAFETY** — HIGH → LOW

**STANDARDS** — LOW → HIGH

### COMFORT ZONE
May be comfortable in the short term but business success is an illusion if problems are swept under the carpet and allowed to fester. Psychological safety is not about "being nice."

### LEARNING AND HIGH-PERFORMANCE ZONE
The ideal state of inclusivity and openness. Allows safe interpersonal risk-taking, fostering innovation, improvement, resilience, and self-development.

### APATHY ZONE
Often characterized by a "dangerous silence," when people have learned that speaking up, even about serious risks, leads to ridicule or retribution.

### ANXIETY ZONE
A blame culture in which failure is stigmatized. Organizations will atrophy and fail to make the most of talent when people are on the defensive.

# Using competences

**How can you define what you need to become an effective leader? You may find some inspiration in the lives of great business, political, and military leaders of the past. But a more reliable way of shaping your objectives is to use competences—descriptions of performance outputs that characterize leadership in your organization.**

## Emulating the greats

Bookshops are lined with the biographies of famous leaders, which tell us how they acted and dealt with adversity. A lesson that emerges from their life stories is that you lead from who you are. To lead effectively, you must be comfortable in your own skin and live a life according to your own principles. As much as you admire Gandhi or Che Guevara, you can't copy them—this will lead to inconsistent behaviors that will be interpreted as indecisiveness or insincerity.

Competences define what **effective performance** as a leader looks like and **help leaders to identify** their development needs

## Setting objective targets

A more realistic way to shape your aims as a leader is through competences. These are short descriptions that set out the behaviors we want to see in ourselves as leaders. Competences define what effective performance as a leader looks like and—through self-assessment and feedback—help leaders to identify their development needs. You can refer to and use a standard set of leadership competences to review your current performance and set objectives, or do research and consult with others to devise your own.

In focus

## BIAS-FREE COMPETENCES

When creating leadership competences for your organization, make sure that the behaviors listed are not biased against any particular group. Research by Catalyst, a nonprofit that supports women in business, shows that senior leaders tend to promote the stereotypically "masculine" leadership traits with which they are already comfortable, such as being results driven, action oriented and problem solving, over stereotypically "feminine" ones, such as being collaborative, consulting, and empathetic. If such unconscious bias goes unchallenged, it creates a vicious cycle where certain groups are disadvantaged and all leaders possess the same limited range of talents. Understand that a diversity of traits is important in leadership and that these can be exhibited by a diversity of people. Consider hiring an expert to review your competences for biased language and diversity.

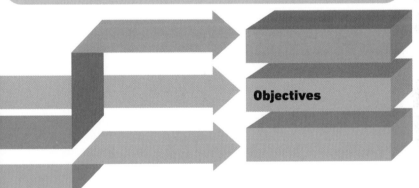

**Objectives**

## Writing your own competences

Using a set of standard competences, such as the ones on the next pages, to define leadership roles may well be appropriate to you. Alternatively, you can identify and list competences by learning from others' experiences—one of the many benefits of joining a professional body for managers or leaders. But the best option is to develop your own competences—ones that accurately target your company's objectives and values.

Understand that a **diversity of traits** is important and that they can be **exhibited** by a diversity of people

## Involving others

When writing competences for leaders, involve a cross-section of people in your organization. Start the discussion with them by asking the question, "What does being effective as a leader look like?" Then invite everyone to make their own contributions to the descriptions of the list of competences in terms that mean something to them.

## Standard leadership competences

| COMPETENCE | DESCRIPTION OF COMPETENCE |
| --- | --- |
| Achieving excellent results | Delivers with **energy and determination** on individual, team, and overall objectives that address **core business issues** and contribute to longer-term organizational goals.<br><br>Behaves in a **professional and ethical** way. |
| Building relationships | Builds trust, listens to needs, is **open to ideas,** and is sensitive to the perceptions of others.<br><br>Questions constructively, identifies options, and **develops solutions** by networking with **strategic people**.<br><br>Is able to work autonomously or in teams, to **adapt to a wide range of situations,** and to appreciate diversity.<br><br>Remains aware of the needs of others and can **focus on objectives and build relationships,** even under pressure or in the face of personal criticism.<br><br>Good at **selecting the right people** with complementary strengths to work in teams. |
| Coaching and communicating | Communicates **a clear vision** of the organization's future.<br><br>Enthuses and **energizes people,** is accessible to people, and gains ownership of the steps needed to achieve goals.<br><br>Knows own and team members' strengths and weaknesses and **encourages initiative** and accountability for objectives.<br><br>Invests in **coaching others,** gives constructive feedback, and knows when to support and challenge.<br><br>Cultivates **good leadership throughout the organization** so that everyone is heard and can contribute; **brings on** the leaders the business will need going forward. |

## Following best practice

Combine the input from your colleagues with the latest research on leadership best practice, and the knowledge you have about the future demands on leaders within the organization. Draft the competences with one eye always on their compatibility with the vision, values, and main strategic objectives and aims of the organization.

| COMPETENCE | DESCRIPTION OF COMPETENCE |
| --- | --- |
| Continuous innovation | Experiments with **new approaches**.<br><br>Learns from best practice, **responds flexibly to change,** and encourages others to question and review how things are done or could be **continuously improved**. |
| Focusing on customers | Achieves **mutually beneficial relationships** with customers.<br><br>**Manages expectations** well in all interactions.<br><br>Anticipates needs and **responds with empathy**. |
| Lifetime learning and knowledge-sharing | Keeps up-to-date, **shares knowledge** and information with other people; applies this learning to own work.<br><br>Encourages others to **learn, develop, and share knowledge**. |
| Solving problems and taking decisions | Recognizes **problems as opportunities,** explores causes systematically and thoroughly.<br><br>Generates ideas; **weighs advantages and disadvantages** of options. |

## Measuring and developing

After you have drafted the competences for a leadership role, you can begin to use them to develop your organization's leaders. The main vehicles for this are formal appraisals and self-assessment:

- Make sure the leader knows and fully understands what the competences are.
- Appoint a "competences advocate"— someone to encourage the leader to use the competences as a development tool.
- Agree the competences to be used in appraisals.
- Train appraisers throughout your organization in the meaning and use of competences.
- Encourage self-assessment against the benchmarks set by the competences.

When being assessed in an appraisal or carrying out self-assessment, it is helpful to recognize four stages of progress toward competence in a given area. So, for example, if you were to assess development in the competence "Solving problems and taking decisions," the results may be as shown below.

## Assessing competences: solving problems

| STAGE OF DEVELOPMENT | ACTIONS DEMONSTRATED |
|---|---|
| NOT YET DEMONSTRATED | Has only recently taken up the current role. |
| DEVELOPING | Finds it difficult to step back from the day-to-day operation and engage with others in **creative problem-solving.** |
| COMPETENT | Encourages other people to put forward new ideas. **Explores systematically** to understand what is happening and why. **Generates ideas to solve problems** and decides on actions. |
| ROLE MODEL/ COACH | **Actively encourages** others to think of problems and tensions as **creative opportunities** to improve service and develop products. |

It is **helpful** to recognize **four stages of progress** toward **competence** in a given area

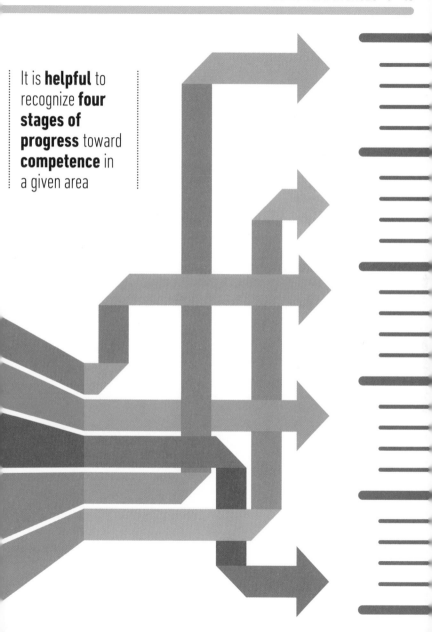

# Providing feedback

**The ability to both give and receive feedback is an essential leadership skill. Giving feedback encourages development and innovative thinking in your team, while knowing how to receive feedback provides an opportunity to learn more about yourself as a leader and the effect your behavior has on others.**

## Opening the dialogue

Giving feedback is not just about telling someone what you think. It is a two-way process that involves listening, asking questions, gaining commitment to change, summarizing what has been covered, and clarifying understanding. Feedback can be given informally in reviews or in quick one-on-one meetings.

Many organizations also provide planned appraisals—regular, formal opportunities for the exchange of feedback, which can include reviews of performance, development, or both. Appraisals happen at least annually and are usually between the line manager

# 85%

of US professionals believe that **feedback** is important to their **development**

## Tip

### CONSIDER YOUR FEEDBACK

View a feedback session as a **learning opportunity.** Even if you are being critical, explain your **point of view** and give suggestions for improvement. Unskilled negative feedback will leave the recipient feeling demotivated, with nothing to build on except their feelings of resentment.

and team member, although they can include others. Feedback from your boss, your team members, peers, and customers is termed "360° feedback;" when segments are omitted (for example, feedback from customers and peers), the term is "180° feedback." Take time to prepare for a feedback session. Book a private room to ensure no interruptions. Always start positively, talk about the recipient's achievements: encourage them to talk about what has gone well. Avoid the tendency to focus more on mistakes they might have made than their strengths; make sure the positive feedback outweighs developmental points you bring up by at least 2:1.

## Avoiding unconscious bias

When conducting appraisals, it's important to be aware of the damaging role that unconscious bias can play. Talented employees can be repeatedly held back, being forced to prove themselves time and again, having their attitude or career ambitions questioned, or getting unfairly pigeonholed as a result of appraisers' subconscious beliefs about their race, gender, age, class, sexuality, or a disability. Research shows that an evidence-based performance evaluation system—and training staff to effectively carry it out—can help level the playing field. Identify the competences valued in each role and oblige appraisers to provide evidence to justify their scores in order to achieve more constructive feedback for all staff members.

## Being specific

Feedback needs to be specific. Deal with one issue at a time rather than try to tackle many issues at once. Be clear and direct in your comments: for example, "The way you gave the information and drew the diagram was really helpful to the customer." General comments, such

**Tip**

**LISTEN FROM AFAR**
There's even greater room for misunderstandings when delivering feedback remotely, so take extra care to be **clear** and direct, to **listen,** and to be open and **receptive.**

as "You were brilliant!" do not give the recipient any opportunities for learning.

Feedback must also be realistic—only refer to actions or behaviors that the person can change. You may have to start with small steps: for example, "It would help if you smiled more when you speak." Gain agreement on small goals, and praise people for reaching the standards you have defined. Skilled feedback gives people information about their behavior and a choice about how and if to act on it—change imposed too heavily invites resistance. Finally, always ask the recipient to summarize the actions they will take as a result of feedback—this helps you to double-check their understanding and commitment to change.

## CHECKLIST...
Preparing to give feedback                                                    YES   NO

1  Are you **clear** on what you want to say? ........................................ ☐ ☐

2  Have you prepared a **positive start** and end to the feedback? ..... ☐ ☐

3  Can you be **specific** in your developmental feedback? ................. ☐ ☐

4  Is this the **best time** to give feedback? .......................................... ☐ ☐

### Giving formal appraisals

When giving a formal appraisal, never show boredom or interrupt. If you find that you are talking more than the person being appraised, rethink your tactics. Use open questions—ones that demand more than a "Yes" or "No" answer—to find out what someone is thinking or feeling. The best questions often start with "What...?" because they make the fewest assumptions about the response, so try:

● What went well?
● What have we learned?

Identify activities and training that will develop the individual in their current role and prepare them for the future. Make clear the business case for any investment in development and training—does it help meet business, team, and individual objectives?

**The best questions** often **start with "What...?"** because they make the fewest assumptions about **the response**

## Getting SMART—setting realistic objectives

| S | M | A |
|---|---|---|
| **SPECIFIC** | **MEASURABLE** | **AGREED** |
| Clearly expressed and within the control of the appraisee. | In terms of quantity, percentage, turnover, or some agreed qualitative measure. | Between the two of you, rather than imposed. |

### Setting SMART objectives

Take time to review the individual's achievements since their last appraisal and establish SMART objectives (see below) for the period until the next appraisal. Agree with them how and when you will measure change. There are many measurement tools at your disposal, including: observation; discussion during appraisals; informal one-on-one reviews; team meetings; examination of business results; other key performance indicators; surveys; and assessment against your organization's competences.

### Closing the appraisal

At the end of the appraisal, it is your turn as leader to ask for any feedback that might be helpful to your working relationship. Be sure to follow up on any support and training you have offered and review progress against agreed milestones. Throughout the year, examine how realistic the standards and deadlines were that you set at the appraisal.

**R**

**REALISTIC**
Challenging but achievable.

**T**

**TIMELY**
With schedules specified.

# 92%
of **organizations** use formal **performance reviews**

# Learning from feedback

**When you seek out and receive feedback, you develop your character as a leader. The two-way process of disclosing things about yourself and receiving comments on your performance builds trust. This in turn reduces the gap between your public and private faces and increases the authenticity of your leadership.**

## Seeking the truth

Once you have learned to both give and receive feedback skillfully and constructively, you will be ready to lead your team into greater self-awareness and higher levels of performance.

You can ask for feedback (formally or informally) from any of the people you come into contact with on a daily basis—members of your team, your superiors, clients, or suppliers.

The following questions are a good starting point for discussion with your appraiser, especially if you ask them to back up their answers with real examples:

- What do you see as my strengths?
- What do you think I am blind to?
- What development areas do you think I should be focusing on?

- What should I do less of/more of?
- What potential do you see in me? Or, if you are using competences to set and monitor your targets, try the following phrasing:
- Which competences do I consistently demonstrate? (Enclose a copy of your competences.)
- Which competences do you think I could go on developing further?
- What changes do you foresee in the next 12 months and on which competences do you think I should be focusing my development?

### In focus

### RUNNING 360° FEEDBACK

Ideally the 360° process should be managed by an objective external coach to ensure high-quality feedback, a balanced viewpoint, and anonymity for those individuals brave enough to give feedback on their boss. However, if your organizational culture is open, and all agree to a no-blame approach, the review could be done internally.

## Becoming a rounded leader

A more formal means of gaining information about yourself—or any individual in your team—from a number of sources is 360° feedback. Ask a selection of four to eight people at different levels in your organization to comment on the leadership behaviors they have seen you displaying over the last year. If appropriate, ask them to consider this against your stated competences.

A questionnaire, set out like a customer satisfaction survey, will help provide a consistent format for the replies.

When you receive feedback from others, compare it with your evaluation of yourself. Which leadership competences are your strengths? Which are your development areas? Which key competences did you find the most challenging last year and which will be even more demanding next year? Note the key development areas and think how you can broaden or deepen your knowledge, skills, or practice—for example reading up on a topic or attending a course. As well as providing valuable insight into others' perceptions of your leadership, 360° feedback is an invaluable tool for helping you prepare for your appraisal discussion with your manager.

**360° feedback** is an invaluable tool for helping you prepare for your **appraisal discussion**

# Developing yourself

**In this action-orientated world, many of us devote insufficient time and energy to our own development. Yet dedicated time for self-development is essential for growing your character and your own individual brand of leadership, as well as the attitudes, skills, and behaviors that will exemplify leadership in others.**

## Reflecting and reviewing

The best way to accelerate your own development and increase awareness of yourself and of others is through regular review and reflection. Put aside an hour every week for self-analysis and contemplation.

Start by reviewing your current development needs. Ask yourself how much of your activity the preceding week contributed to achieving your stated vision and objectives. Next, look at your future development needs and assess your progress against your stated leadership competences. Finally, consider the ideas you have for the next steps in your career; are you honing the skills now that you know will be needed for your career progress?

### Tip

**LISTEN TO YOURSELF**
Review your own progress by questioning yourself: are you building on your strengths and minimizing your weaknesses? Are you **training** your team and delegating to them **successfully?** Are you scheduling time to develop **key relationships?**

### In focus

**YOUR LONG-TERM DEVELOPMENT**
As you mature as a leader, you will need to undertake weekly reviews of your own development and achievements. But you should also take time to think about your long-term goals, and your progress toward them. How well are you living up to your life principles? How have you dealt with disappointment and adversity? Do you ever find yourself questioning your ability to do what's expected of you professionally (the so-called "impostor syndrome")? Have you managed to increase your level of performance? Have you fulfilled commitments to yourself and others? Are you happy in your career? What are your next steps?

The more you learn, the more you realize you still have to learn. At this point, you might consider seeking advice from a career counselor.

## Journaling

Great leaders possess self-awareness and character—attributes acquired through reflection and self-analysis, but also through dealing regularly with real-life situations. Using a private journal to write down what you have learned about yourself in your day-to-day life can be very helpful. Record, for example, how you have helped someone else develop and learn, and how this has honed your own strengths as a leader.

Use your journal to make personal observations about how you respond to different conditions—what happens when you are tired or stressed? The journal can help you record and work through relationships that you are enjoying or struggling with, and to reflect on the highs and lows of your moods that you could not reveal in the workplace.

At first, journaling may seem a chore; and initially your journal may not contain many connections or life-lessons. But after a number of weeks, you'll find that journaling becomes a habit that gives structure to your review and thinking time. Looking back over your journal will reveal how your leadership has developed, how you can trust yourself, even in difficult situations, and what the recurring issues are.

> Assess your **progress** against your **leadership competences**

**Tip**

### KEEP YOUR FEET ON THE GROUND
Never become so grand that you lose touch with what it feels like to work with a customer on a project or to make a sale. Recognize that your role is now to **help others enjoy** this too.

## ASK YOURSELF...
About your development needs

|  | | YES | NO |
|---|---|---|---|
| **1** | Are your most time-consuming tasks related to processes? Do you need to **develop time-** or project-management skills, or planning abilities? | ☐ | ☐ |
| **2** | Are your most time-consuming tasks related to **content?** Do you need to address a lack of knowledge in areas such as marketing, finance, sales, or IT? | ☐ | ☐ |
| **3** | Are your most time-consuming tasks related to people? Do you need **training** in recruitment, motivation, teambuilding, coaching, or delegating? | ☐ | ☐ |

# Balancing work and life

**Most people would say that they want to be healthy, happy, and make a valued contribution at work to a successful organization. Creating and maintaining this sense of well-being is an integral part of your role as a leader. It involves taking a measured view of the balance between work and life and having realistic expectations of your team.**

## Attending to different needs

Good leaders know their team, their capabilities, and what motivates them. The real skill, though, is being able to use this knowledge to balance the needs of the task, the team, and its individual members. Maintaining this equilibrium is not always easy, because emphasis inevitably shifts from one area to another. For example, bursts of intense effort may be needed to meet tight deadlines—fine once in a while, but exhausting on a regular basis. Similarly, switching to remote working brings work-life balance benefits, but can also add pressure to be available at all hours, increasing stress.

**Tip**

### ACCENTUATE THE POSITIVE

Promote a **healthy work–life balance** and you'll not only avoid the pitfalls of stress and burnout in your team, but generate **real benefits** to the business. **Happy** staff deliver better results and empathetic customer service; and staff retention and recruitment then becomes easier.

## Avoiding burnout

Left unmanaged, chronic work stress leads to burnout, something to avoid as it has no easy fix. Workers who experience burnout—characterized by exhaustion, a cynicism toward work, and a lack of efficacy—often have to change careers, draining your pool of available talent.

## CHECKLIST...
Achieving balance in your life

|  | YES | NO |
|---|:---:|:---:|
| **1** I often buy new books and **have time to read** them | ☐ | ☐ |
| **2** People remark on how **open** I am to **new ideas** | ☐ | ☐ |
| **3** I have a **regular exercise** routine | ☐ | ☐ |
| **4** I usually get a **good night's sleep** | ☐ | ☐ |
| **5** I have **enough energy** to see me through each day | ☐ | ☐ |
| **6** I **express** my feelings | ☐ | ☐ |
| **7** I know who I am and that's **fine** | ☐ | ☐ |
| **8** I have a **clear sense of purpose** in my life and make a real contribution at work | ☐ | ☐ |

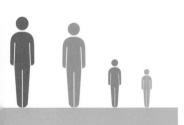

You may need to invest time in **team meetings** and **calm tensions** to **maintain balance**

### Managing stress
Your goal should be to keep your team members stretched and working to their best ability, but not stressed. Ensure everyone has regular and predictable time off. If you have built a strong team during good times, it will withstand short-term pressures, but you may need to invest time in team meetings and calm tensions to maintain balance. Stresses are cumulative: a team member may be able to tolerate stress at work for a while if other aspects of their life are running well. But if work stress is only one of many issues they are dealing with, problems may arise that you should acknowledge.

If you're leading a remote team, set limits on work time and share them with staff to maintain boundaries between your job and personal life. For example, stop checking work messages after hours and respect flexible working arrangements.

# Inspiring and encouraging

**From the way they formulate and express their overarching vision to the thought they put into everyday interactions—the glue of any team relationship—good leaders encourage and inspire others around them at every level of activity.**

## Setting a good example

One of the basic rules of leadership is that in order to inspire others you must aspire to be a model of excellence yourself. Of course, your personal journey toward excellence will never end, but it will give you two vital qualities—the desire to learn, and, in turn, that will lead to the humility of knowing how much more you have to learn.

Your role is about providing inspiration, and that starts with a clear vision for a better future, which you will need to communicate to your team on a daily basis through your words and actions:

- Make it clear to others that they have the capability and power to make a difference—that their unique attributes can help achieve the vision.
- Bring hope for the future to sustain people through change and adversity; if people feel overwhelmed and slow down, bring them back to the vision with simple messages that show the next small steps forward.
- Point out progress made and signs of success on the way to fill people once again with confidence and the desire to go forward.
- Praise new ideas and the courage demonstrated in new ventures.
- Keep team members stretched— one step ahead of what they thought they could do.
- Keep positive: explain that most experiments that do not work are not failures—just feedback; turn setbacks into positive impetus for change.

**How to inspire through your vision**

**Your role** is about providing **inspiration**, and that starts with a clear vision for a better **future**

State your vision in **highly positive terms**

## BEING POSITIVE

| Dos | Don'ts |
| --- | --- |
| O **Telling someone you enjoy working with them** | O Complaining to someone that you feel tired or ill |
| O **Smiling at people—sincerely, with your eyes** | O Being too shy to enjoy life or try new things |
| O **Thanking others for honest feedback** | O Excusing your falling standards |
| O **Controlling your emotions** | O Demotivating others just because you feel demotivated |

## Taking opportunities

Think how many opportunities you have in a single day to interact with your team, colleagues, bosses, and other stakeholders. Over 100 contacts a day—by phone, email, face-to-face, etc.—is not unusual for today's busy leaders and managers. Every one of these interactions, however brief, is an opportunity to encourage, inspire, and make your leadership felt.

When you make every meeting count, you create thousands of potential advocates for you, your team, your vision, and your organization. Moments add up to real commercial gain.

> **Tip**
>
> **ZAP, DON'T SAP**
> At every meeting, give people a zap—a **quick burst** of **positive energy**—and avoid the sap—anything that leaves them discouraged.

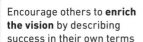

Encourage others to **enrich the vision** by describing success in their own terms

**Contextualize the vision**— describe when, where, and with whom it will be achieved

## Focusing on the now

Inspiring people is less about delivering impassioned speeches and having a forceful personality, and more about focus and consistency. Treat everyone you deal with as a valued customer. Place them at the center of your universe for the duration of any interaction you have.

Give them your full attention whether you are speaking face-to-face or on the phone. Be dependable in your daily interactions: your consistency builds trust and peace of mind in your team members, freeing them to focus on their key tasks rather than worrying about you.

# Leading through
# **challenges**

In business, change is a constant. Organizations are forever having to adapt to new realities and create opportunities for growth—something that's truer than ever in today's fast-shifting "new normal." It is your role as a leader to steer the changes, encouraging others to take on new challenges, and project credibility and integrity even in times of uncertainty.

03

# Focusing on the future

**As a leader, you'll need to make tough decisions, plan a course of action, and take your team with you. The best way to achieve this is to involve your team from the start; explain what criteria your judgement is based upon and how plans are connected to other activities in the organization.**

## Making decisions

Leaders set the agenda in three key areas—determining the direction in which the organization will move, shaping how the organization does business, and setting the pace of change. Decisions you make in any of these three key areas should be based on objective criteria; research shows that an evidence-based approach—in which decisions are made using evidence and critical thinking—is more effective than simply relying on personal experience, conventional wisdom, or anecdote. Test your decision by assessing its strengths, weaknesses, opportunities, and threats (SWOT).

## Locating change

Deciding which opportunities to explore, exploit, and reject requires a crystal clear understanding of your organization's purpose and mission. In particular, you must know what gives your business its edge over the competition and use this knowledge to guide your future focus. Competitive advantage is based on what customers value and the organization's strengths relative to the competition. It takes into account external trends that will help or hinder momentum. In a SWOT analysis, internal factors are strengths and weaknesses, while external issues are opportunities and threats.

## ASK YOURSELF...
What's our competitive advantage?                                          YES  NO

1  Do we know what **business** we are not in? ...................................... ☐ ☐

2  Do we know our **core values**? .............................................. ☐ ☐

3  Do we know what **business** we are in? ......................................... ☐ ☐

4  Do we differentiate ourselves by offering our customers
   **unique benefits**? ................................................................. ☐ ☐

5  Do we differentiate ourselves by offering our customers
   **better prices**? ..................................................................... ☐ ☐

## Question your decisions using a SWOT analysis

### S

### STRENGTHS
- What **advantages** or **unique ideas and proposals** do you have?
- What do you do differently or **better than anyone else?**
- What **unusual materials or low-cost resources** do you have sole access to?
- How can you build **organizational resilience?**

### W

- Weaknesses
- What challenges or areas should you avoid?
- Do new products or processes need **further development or investment?**
- Have market research results been **positive, or is there insufficient demand?**

### O

### OPPORTUNITIES
- What emerging opportunities or **trends** can you identify?
- What interesting **changes in technology** and developing products are you aware of?
- Are there new **consumer spending patterns** or demand for different services?
- How can investing in **analytics** help you identify opportunities?

### T

### THREATS
- Are stringent **quality requirements** being imposed?
- Are you in a **financial position** to adapt to change quickly?
- Would any communication or technological issue **challenge your market position?**
- **How can you recognize risks earlier?**
- **And how can you be ready for the risks you can't foresee?**

## Keeping objective

A weighted assessment will make clear the criteria you can use to make a decision and give your decision transparency. In this simple example (right), a decision has to be made to adopt one of two projects—A or B; both seem attractive and have similar costs. To carry out the assessment, first engage with your team to make a list of criteria that the projects should satisfy. Not all criteria are of equal importance, so give each one a score from 1 to 10 depending on how valuable the team considers it to be. Check that the criteria are rounded—not all skewed toward finance, for example. Score each option (A and B) out of 10 on each criterion, and multiply each score by its corresponding weighting. Add the scores to see which project fulfils the criteria best.

Not all **criteria** are of equal importance, so give each one **a score from 1 to 10** depending on **how valuable** the team considers it to be

| Weighted assessment |
| --- |
| CRITERIA |
| Maximize long-term customer satisfaction |
| Maximize return on investment |
| Maximize sustainability |
| Maximize high quality standards |
| Maximize long-term profit potential |
| Maximize staff satisfaction |
| Maximize added value for customers |
| Minimize hassle and administrative complexity |
| Maximize fun and interesting work |
| TOTAL |

| WEIGHTING | SCORE PLAN A | PLAN A x WEIGHTING | SCORE PLAN B | PLAN B x WEIGHTING |
|---|---|---|---|---|
| 10 | 6 | 60 | 9 | 90 |
| 9 | 5 | 45 | 4 | 36 |
| 8 | 9 | 72 | 4 | 32 |
| 8 | 6 | 48 | 10 | 80 |
| 8 | 8 | 64 | 5 | 40 |
| 7 | 2 | 14 | 10 | 70 |
| 7 | 6 | 42 | 8 | 56 |
| 5 | 10 | 50 | 7 | 35 |
| 4 | 3 | 12 | 8 | 32 |
| | | **407** | | **471** |

## Setting the pace

When orchestrating strategic change within an organization, you need to give careful consideration to timing. If the rate of change is too slow, the process may simply run out of momentum; if it is too fast, you risk creating stress and burnout.

Aim for a sustainably fast pace at which your major initiatives will have started to produce measurable results within a year—even if the whole process is scheduled to take much longer. Steering significant organizational change is hard work: typically, there is a trough in visible results just at the point where you need the most effort and commitment from all stakeholders. Investors, in particular, may lose heart in this trough period, so need to be reminded regularly of the benefits to come.

Plan in "quick wins" throughout the process of change—achievements that have high visibility but require little effort. Celebrate and publicize these successes, and drip-feed messages about how project milestones and results achieved so far are bringing the vision nearer to reality.

Aim for **a sustainably fast pace** at which your **major initiatives** will have **started** to produce **measurable results** within a year

**Connected organizational plans**

**Strategic Business Plan**

**Tip**

**OPEN CHANNELS**
Keep **listening** to everyone you are connected to; **share ideas,** and keep **open channels of communication** that are needed now and may be needed in the future.

# 96%

of organizations are in some **phase of transformation**

## Integrating change

Everything in an organization is connected. Processes and systems in one area impact on others. As a leader, you should make explicit the connections between different plans and explain how each one contributes to the vision. Understanding the bigger picture will help your team to recognize their role and commit to change. The message can be a complex one, so communicate little and often, and check in regularly to see how well people have understood the connections between plans, departments, and roles.

**Human Resources and Organization Development Plan**

**Operations Plan (products and services)**

**Finance, IT Sourcing, and R & D Plans**

**Marketing Plan**

# Enabling change

**Opportunities for innovation exist at every level of an organization, and leaders must continuously plan change to move forward and stay ahead of competitors. Processes, systems, skills, and competences can always be improved, or the whole business can be moved in an entirely new direction. Leading change requires a sense of balance between priorities and keen awareness of responses among all stakeholders.**

## Balancing priorities

A key leadership skill is keeping a good balance between short-term improvement and long-term innovation. If you are continuously improving at the margins while neglecting strategic innovation, it will lead to organizational myopia and the risk of missing out on the next big trend. Conversely, constant innovation at the core can become counterproductive because people will eventually feel worn out and unwilling to take on yet another new initiative.

## Maintaining stability

The leader seeks to progress with both short- and long-term change while maintaining equilibrium. This can be a challenge: while most people will quickly accommodate small steps that visibly improve the way things are done, bold strategic innovation requires the leader to inspire people, sometimes for many years, before seeing a return. Before implementing change, discuss its implications with multiple small groups of stakeholders. People should feel free to ask questions and express their concerns. Help people to see what will remain the same—these things can provide an anchor of stability for those who dislike change.

## How to recognize the stages of adaptation to change

**Expectation:** anticipation and excitement

**Standstill:** numbness, disorientation, denial

**Lack of energy:** missing "the old days"

## Reacting to change

People react differently to change. At one extreme are the innovators who may be so eager about walking toward a new future that they fail to realize no one has followed them. At the other end are the stragglers, who join in only when everyone else has moved on. Traditionalists hang on to the past, viewing change as a threat. Surprisingly, they have one thing in common with the innovators—they respond to the impending change with emotion. The remainder—the cautious majority—are likely to weigh the arguments put across.

**Tip**

**EXPECT DISSENT**
When you introduce **high-level change,** expect at least 50 percent of your people to hate the idea.

**Low output:** feelings of loss, the need to let go, detachment from others

**Incompetence:** depression, apathy, resentment

**Increasing energy:** gradual acceptance of the new reality

**Conflict in the team:** resistance, anger, arguing

**Problem-solving:** exploring the new situation and ideas, experimenting, hope

## Adjusting to plans

As leader, you need to use both logic and emotion when explaining your plans. Be persistent and emphasize to everyone the benefits to come when the changes have been made.

People take different lengths of time to adjust to change and you should prepare for the long haul: typically, the adjustment process falls into distinct phases, which are characterized by different sets of behaviors. Be aware that people who adopt change quickly can show impatience with the slowest; this can lead to conflict within the team, which you may be called upon to help resolve.

**Increased effectiveness:** search for new purpose, commitment to new situation

**Productivity:** reengagement, commitment, motivation

# Energizing the team

**When you assemble a group of people—whether it's two or several thousand—you don't automatically get a team. For that to happen, the group must be energized, focused, and view success as a collective rather than individual aim. Your job as a leader is to create that transformation.**

## Choosing your team

Selecting team members who work together well, motivating the group, and dealing with conflict are the essential aspects of team leadership. And as increasing amounts of work are project-based, you need to develop team cohesion and focus quickly despite rapid changes in the mix of the team. This is even harder if you have team members working remotely, so ensuring that everyone can contribute ideas and access data equally is paramount.

Invest time at the start of a project to choose or strengthen the team—your investment will be repaid when the pressure rises. Pick team members with complementary skills that will come into play at different stages of a project. Your team should have a good mix of the thinking styles listed below. If the team is small, members may have to fill more than one role.

**The leader**—ensures everyone understands the objectives; motivates and communicates.

**The creative**—an imaginative thinker who has bold concepts at the outset of a project and provides ideas when the team is stuck.

**The analyst**—the problem-solver who tests the plan at every stage.

**The facilitator**—has good interpersonal skills, is sensitive to the group dynamic, and acts as the "glue" in a team.

**The administrator**—pays attention to details and keeps the team on time and focused on the task.

**Leader**

**Creative**

**Analyst**

**Facilitator**

**Administrator**

**Tip**

**BE INCLUSIVE**
**Welcome** newcomers to the team and **encourage** them to speak at meetings and engage with the group from an early stage. Don't allow new recruits to become accustomed to a backseat role.

## Running your team

Make clear the roles that each individual will play in the team. Devolve decision-making to the group as far as possible, and encourage everyone to participate in decisions—this will share the ownership of goals. Set out shared values, develop ground rules that describe how the team will work together from the start, and watch the way that group dynamics develop. Take action immediately at the first sign of conflict or if an individual starts to act in a way not consistent with the agreed team rules.

When you build and manage your team successfully, **group members** will make one another **accountable** for achieving individual tasks, and begin to **appreciate collective success**

## The signs of an energized team

Showing commitment

Listening

Sharing

Getting results

Showing interest

Building trust

Giving recognition

# 21%

greater **profitability** is shown by **highly engaged** teams

## Building trust

Be supportive, give credit for good cooperative work and knowledge shared, and always promote and celebrate team achievements.

When you build and manage your team successfully, group members will start to make one another accountable for achieving individual tasks, and begin to appreciate and share in collective success. Trust will build gradually as each member commits to actions at team meetings and carries them out as promised.

Innovating

Supporting one another

Giving constructive feedback

Being trusting, honest, and open

Collaborating

Taking risks

# Managing conflict

**Building a successful team depends on cooperation between all members of the group. But what if some people won't play ball? Unproductive confrontations with you as leader or between team members can take up a lot of your time, create a bad atmosphere, and stop you from achieving your aims, so finding positive ways to deal with disagreement is a key leadership skill.**

## Dealing with conflict

Conflict arises when people stop listening and approach a situation from their own point of view. As leader, you must look beyond the confrontation to understand what it is really happening and discover the roots of the hostility.

Begin with yourself: your role means you may be a factor in a team member's dissatisfaction. Differences in outlook, behavior, and style can lead to tension—which can be used constructively to stimulate creativity and enrich the team or, if left unmanaged, can cause division.

## Meeting standards

It is tempting to work around conflict, but this undermines the team and your position as leader. You should explore all courses of action to bring about improvement. But many people find adversarial situations hard and may sabotage their own future if they do not see a way out. If open discussion and support fails to achieve changes, you will need to work within your organization's disciplinary policy and procedures to deal with the situation, and prevent an adverse effect on the rest of the team.

## ASK YOURSELF...
Is it me?                                                                      YES   NO

1  Have I explained **new initiatives** clearly—could they be causing insecurity or anxiety? ...................................................... ☐ ☐

2  Do I come across as **approachable** and **accessible**? ..................... ☐ ☐

3  Have I made unreasonable demands? ............................................ ☐ ☐

4  Have I been **fair** in my praise or my criticism? ............................. ☐ ☐

5  Am I portraying the **right image** for a leader? ............................. ☐ ☐

## Why conflict arises

| CAUSE | EFFECT | REMEDY |
|---|---|---|
| **Reaching the limits of current capability** | Team member **makes errors** and cannot do the job to the **required standard.** Other team members become impatient. | Offer **support and training** over a reasonable timescale. If there is little improvement, their future in your team is limited. |
| **Becoming disengaged** | **Rejection of the job;** withdrawal from involvement with the team. Often caused by frustration when high achievers have been held back over time. Will have **an adverse effect** on the entire team. | Explore causes in a **one-on-one discussion.** If you have inherited this team member, you need to release the burden of all the past broken promises and **build new trust.** Consider counseling. |
| **Getting distracted** | **Focus moves elsewhere,** reducing effectiveness. The cause is often personal and while colleagues will sympathize initially, they will soon get tired of the issue. | Listen sympathetically and **arrange time off** if you think this will help to solve the problem. Make sure that you recognize when the problem goes beyond your ability and ask for additional help. |
| **Losing motivation** | Too little or too much delegation or challenge in the role can bring about **demotivation and decreased effectiveness.** The team member can quickly have a negative effect on team morale. | Get to know what particularly **motivates each member of the team.** Ask yourself if you are over- or under-delegating to the person. Over-delegation can cause paralyzing fear of failure. |

# Balancing targets

**Results are what it's all about. They are the synthesis of all your thinking, planning, and enabling as a leader. To get what you want from a project, you should clarify standards and objectives from the outset. Your targets need to be realistic, and they also require a means of measuring the performance of all involved.**

## Getting the right results

The targets you set for your team should challenge everyone but also be realistic, in line with the SMART criteria (see pp.46–47). Ensure the aims you set are balanced; as well as financial targets, include goals in areas such as speed of response, product and service quality, customer and team satisfaction, and brand development. List the desired results in each of four key areas—customers, operations, people, and finance—so that no one objective takes assumed priority over another. Review results in each area monthly so that you can prove progress to yourself, your team, and your investors.

**CUSTOMERS**

- O Customer service staff motivated
- O Customers satisfied
- O Customer experience enjoyable
- O Lifetime loyalty promoted

# 140%

more money is likely to be spent by customers who enjoy **positive service experiences**

## Setting service-level agreements

Clarify the results you expect from interactions between purchasers and providers or between departments in a service-level agreement. You can then present the obligations in a written format—minimum or maximum standards and timescales, or other measures of reliability or availability, for example:

- Our obligations: to provide you with information within four hours of request, etc.
- Your obligations: to respond to service requests within four hours of phone call enquiry, etc.

## KEEPING MULTIPLE TARGETS IN PLAY

### PEOPLE

- O Perception of being a good employer
- O Personal development
- O Mutual respect fostered
- O Interesting work

### OPERATIONS

- O Stocks delivered to warehouse in time
- O Safe working throughout
- O Delivery to customer as promised
- O Competitive prices

### FINANCE

- O Profits
- O Investment
- O Sales
- O Cash

List the **desired results** in each of four key areas—**customers, operations, people, and finance**

# Improving confidence

**Confidence is a cornerstone of good leadership. Especially in times of uncertainty, upheaval, or crisis, believing in yourself and making the right decisions will give you credibility and integrity, which in turn will enhance the organization's reputation and build trust in all stakeholders.**

## Being prepared

Confidence can come in a number of different ways. It comes from experience as your track record as a leader improves. It comes from having well-formed plans and anticipating challenges, and it comes from the knowledge that you have a strong business built on productive working relationships.

**Tip**

**BOOST YOURSELF**
Regularly **affirm** your own **strengths** as a leader by privately listing your **abilities and achievements.** This will give you an instant **confidence boost** and banish that internal critic living in your head.

### COMMUNICATING WITH CONFIDENCE
While there are no shortcuts to building confidence, there are ways that you can project confidence to your team and to your stakeholders.

O **Use confident language** to describe your vision. Listen and learn from political leaders, who characteristically employ optimistic language that suggests a future state—words such as "innovative," "special," "original," "latest," "breakthrough," "updated," and "leading-edge." Used regularly, this kind of vocabulary spreads through the organization.

O **Deliver your vision** messages in soundbites no more than 30 seconds long that sum up the benefits of the opportunities you wish to explore.

O **Use the right nonverbal signals**—communication is about more than what you say. Adopting a relaxed posture, using small gestures kept close to your body, speaking at a firm volume, smiling, and making plenty of eye contact all help project confidence and calmness.

## CHECKLIST...
Staying calm in adversity

**YES**  **NO**

1 Do I know what **triggers** an emotional overreaction in me? ......... ☐ ☐

2 Can I **spot** the signs of stress in myself? ...................................... ☐ ☐

3 Am I able to delay my **response** for a few seconds before
I respond? ..................................................................................... ☐ ☐

## Acknowledging ideas

Your inner confidence will grow when you behave in a confident manner and gain the trust of your team and colleagues. An ability and willingness to devolve power and decision-making is one vital characteristic that marks a confident leader, so take every opportunity to involve others and empower them to act on their ideas. Be open about what is not working for you, your customers, suppliers, or employees; your frankness will be interpreted as an expression of confidence because you approach success and adversity with equal zeal. Encourage people to discover and understand situations for themselves rather than spoon-feeding them issues and answers—remember, your power increases as you give it away.

> Take every opportunity to **involve others** and empower them to act on their **ideas**—your power **grows** as you give it away

**Tip**

**FACE YOUR FEARS**
**Confidence** comes from **self-knowledge;** understanding your thoughts and actions gives you the ability to control them.
A good way to become more **self-assured** is to face your fears—do that presentation, confront your difficult CEO, and reply to that demanding client now.

## Being consistent

As a leader, your every word and action is scrutinized by your team and could be given far more significance than you intended. Perceptions of you as a confident leader can be undermined by conscious or unconscious slips, so try to think in a measured way about the kind of signals you are sending out. Consistency and calmness in adversity are characteristics that most people will perceive as confidence.

# Creating networks

**As a leader, you will need to create, develop, and maintain networks of contacts within and far beyond your own organization. Networks enable you to exchange information with others, share resources, gain referrals, leads, or recommendations, test ideas, build long-term relationships, and help others in return.**

## Reaping the rewards

Networks are your eyes and ears. They warn you about trends and developments in markets, signal opportunities and threats, and help identify niches for you to exploit. So, the wider your network becomes, the more responsive you will be to any market changes.

## Contributing to networks

Building effective networks can take a few months or a few years; maintaining them takes a lifetime. Digital communication tools, from social media sites such as LinkedIn, to video calls and virtual networking events, now make that easier—and more global—than ever. But remember that networking is a two-way process: the more you give to others, the more you gain. People will quickly categorize you as a "taker" if you only get in touch when you want something. Engage and offer help before you need it yourself. Introducing a contact to someone you think they should know, posting interesting information online, and making insightful comments about others' posts are all good ways of being useful, sparking conversations, and building relationships.

### Tip

**CONNECT**
To network effectively on sites such as LinkedIn, start by **filling out** your entire profile (including a **photo**). Send **personalized messages** to make connections, then **build relationships** by sharing and writing content, and commenting. Also **join relevant groups**—or set up your own.

## How to build an effective network

**List all potentially** useful contacts and ask your team to do the same

**Include former** workplaces and colleagues and personal contacts of family and friends

## **Attending events**

While digital networking helps expand your contacts, you can make stronger connections face to face. Business associations and professional bodies often run specific networking events, but any meeting with colleagues, clients, or suppliers is a chance to network. At any event, take time to gauge the etiquette—more often it's about socializing, with business follow-ups the next day. Try to talk in-depth with two or three people with potential to help you rather than working the entire room, and always follow up the next day with anything promised. Suggest a way to collaborate that might be of mutual benefit—don't pitch for business unless the event is designed for that.

**Keep in touch** regularly and always follow up on promises

**Think creatively** about what you can offer to help your network contacts in return

**Review your list** sector by sector to remind yourself of people. Find them on networking sites

**85%** of all **jobs** are filled via **networking**

## NETWORKING IN PERSON

### Dos

- O **Preparing some introductory questions or ice-breakers**
- O **Introducing yourself clearly, briefly, and memorably**
- O **Leaving a physical gap in your group that invites someone to join**
- O **Suggesting to exchange contact info**

### Don'ts

- O Forgetting to study the guest list
- O Not researching the people you would like to meet
- O Mismatching what you say with your body language
- O Barging into groups with no eye contact first

# Learning from entrepreneurs

**Entrepreneurs enjoy creating value by taking advantage of opportunities and solving problems for customers. Leaders in organizations of all sizes—and in all markets—can learn from their bold approach: it is just a question of looking at old problems in new ways and producing innovative solutions.**

## Finding opportunities

What defines entrepreneurs is their preparedness to listen to their customers, see new opportunities, and back their ideas with drive and determination. They also have a refreshing attitude to "failure"—everything is viewed as a useful experience, and trial and error is seen as a legitimate path to success. Entrepreneurs think ahead, don't accept the status quo, and ask questions that begin with "why?," "why not?," and "what if...?."

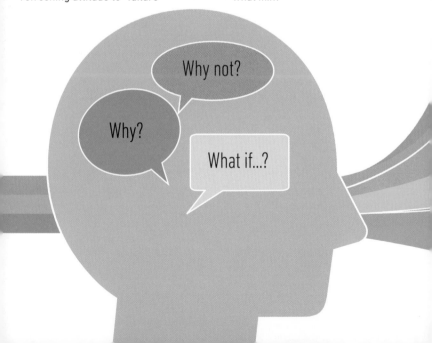

# 49%

greater productivity is
achieved in firms created
by **serial entrepreneurs**

How can we help you? Celebrate
both **successes and failures** as
**signs of entrepreneurship,** and be
sure to **reward** the contributions
people make to creating value for the
business, and responding flexibly to
opportunities to solve problems for
customers. Scrutinize your business
for **new opportunities.** Think hard,
and above all, **think creatively.**

Large corporations are increasingly
encouraging their leaders to show
**entrepreneurial zeal** within the
mature organization—a phenomenon
called **intrapreneurship.**

Looking at your business with
an **entrepreneurial mindset**
will help you generate ideas for
maximizing **opportunities for
growth** that no one else has
seen—either within or outside
the organization.

Embrace **uncertainty** like an
entrepreneur. Don't be afraid
to take **calculated risks,** and
accept your failures as
learning experiences. Doing
**nothing** is the only approach
destined to eventually fail.

Develop your own
**entrepreneurial
leadership skills** by
asking more questions
of customers and
colleagues—what issues
cause you regular hassle?

## Developing entrepreneurial skills

Entrepreneurs exhibit many important traits and crucial skills that you can examine and develop in yourself to benefit your own organization. Most entrepreneurs are risk-takers, goal-focused, and determined—all traits you can learn. When looking for new ideas, examine your own organization first: can you exploit existing assets? In a fast-changing world, is your organization able to adapt quickly? As you search outside your company for emerging trends and products, remember to apply SWOT criteria to test and assess your decisions (see pp.58–59).

### Where to look for entrepreneurial ideas

#### UNDERUTILIZED INFORMATION OR ASSETS

O Can we sell our **information** externally?

O Can we get **better performance** by outsourcing?

O Can we **lease** our assets?

O Can we repackage our assets using **emerging technology** to create new products?

#### WAYS TO CHANGE THE BUSINESS MODEL

O Will acquisitions **boost** our **capabilities?**

O Can we cut out the middle-man?

O Should we **support** employee spin-offs?

O Can we replace on-premises solutions with more cost-effective **cloud-based** ones?

**Tip**

**HARNESS TALENT**
You may have a **natural entrepreneur** already in your team. Give them the space to **innovate** and put up with their often challenging nature and you will gain a real asset.

# 35%

of US workers are only given time to think **creatively** a few times a year

## NEW MARKETS, NEW CUSTOMERS

O Can we **change** our pricing structures?

O Can we do what we do for our **best customers** for others?

O How do we **extend** our markets?

O Can we use **customer data** to increase sales?

## NEW PRODUCTS AND SERVICES

O Can we **sell our products** or services as a system?

O Can we turn internal services into **sales?**

O Can we **meet** unmet needs?

O Can we use reporting and **analytics** to create new products and services?

# Developing
# **leaders**

By discovering and developing up-and-coming leadership talent, today's leaders play a vital role in the future of organizations across the world. Doing this effectively requires an inclusive approach and an organizational culture that fosters leadership at all levels and across all employees. Get it right, and the result is a legacy that will live on in generations of future leaders.

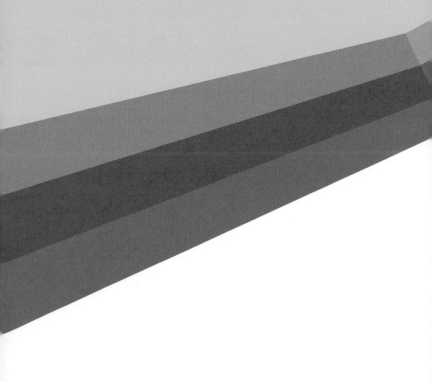

04

# Investing in the future

**For an organization to expand, it needs to invest in developing the new leaders who will take it forward. Individuals who display leadership potential should be considered important assets who will grow if nurtured, and be lost if not.**

### Appointing talent

A successful organization needs a ready supply of new leaders. Recruiting all future leaders from outside of your organization simply isn't cost effective: it takes a substantial amount of management time and money to find the right candidates and bring them up to speed. By contrast, leaders who are promoted from within your organization already have a good understanding of its culture and working methods, and will have been nurtured and trained by you to have exactly the suite of skills and knowledge required to take on their new role.

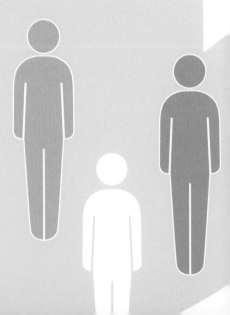

**SPOT THE SIGNS OF CHANGE**
Train yourself as a **leader** to recognize the **signs of transition** between different stages of **leadership,** and be ready to support individuals as they push for the **next level.**

# 30%

of organizations say they are effectively **developing leaders** to meet evolving challenges

## Realizing potential

One of your key goals as a leader is to recognize leadership qualities in others, and to know how to encourage and assist future leaders so they can realize their full potential. Take a long-term approach to developing talent, rather than filling positions as they arise, creating organizational structures and cultures that foster and enable leaders. You might even consider implementing a distributed leadership model, empowering any team member to lead if required. To ensure you are developing talent across the board, use an evidence-based appraisal system to combat unconscious bias (see pp.44–45).

It can be helpful to think of leadership growing as a series of transitions in self-awareness, skill, and responsibility. Recognizing these crucial changes in others, and responding appropriately, will help to accelerate the development of new leaders. Each stage on the path to leadership brings challenges—both in terms of taking on new responsibilities and leaving behind old behaviors. This can be a stressful time for new leaders, who may feel overwhelmed just when they are expected to shine. They are unlikely to be comfortable raising their concerns with you, their manager, for fear of looking like they are failing.

## How to help potential leaders make transitions

Identify the individual's **current stage** of leadership

**Potential leaders** start taking on more responsibility and begin **questioning** the ways things are done

Others in the organization start to **recognize their vision**

**Help them identify** what they needed to let go of to reach this stage

---

### CHECKLIST...

Creating future leaders in your organization | **YES** | **NO**

1 Do you look for **win–win situations** for you/your team/other teams/the organization? □ □

2 Do you demonstrate **good stewardship** of talent for the whole organization's benefit? □ □

3 Do you have a **track record** of unselfishly releasing potential leaders to take up development opportunities? □ □

4 Do you **initiate** the development of potential leaders? □ □

5 Do you **encourage** members of your team to apply for internal promotion or transfers? □ □

## Recognizing leadership stages

The first sign of leadership potential is the transition from being self-focused and performing your individual role to a high standard to becoming more aware of, and helpful to, others. Potential leaders then start taking on more responsibility and begin questioning the ways things are done and coming up with ideas for doing things differently.

As a potential leader develops, others in the organization start to recognize their vision and that they have a talent for spotting important opportunities that will benefit the team or the organization as a whole. Potential leaders thrive on added responsibility, and when they have a team to manage, they contribute at a higher level, working well with their peers, and showing a talent for developing team members. Other staff members naturally gravitate toward them to sound out ideas—a process that may develop into more formal mentoring or coaching roles. Ultimately, they start to develop the skills needed to nurture the next generation of leaders in your organization.

**Ask them** what they do differently now that they are at this stage

# 94%

of organizations plan to **increase** or maintain their current **leadership development** spending

**Decide** between you the areas you would like to develop next

When they have a **team to manage,** they contribute at **a higher level**

**Identify role models** who could help them make the next transition

## Making leadership transitions

| STATE OF LEADERSHIP | TAKING UP THE NEW | LETTING GO OF THE OLD |
|---|---|---|
| SELF-AWARENESS | O Doing more than the job description<br>O Performing excellently<br>O Accepting more responsibility<br>O Inheriting corporate memory<br>O Becoming a team player<br>O Suggesting improvements | O Doing the job description<br>O Keeping yourself to yourself<br>O Focusing on your own performance<br>O Carrying out everything to the letter<br>O Referring to "I" |
| OTHER-AWARENESS | O Greater empathy<br>O Helping fellow workers<br>O Being diplomatic<br>O Looking for win–win solutions<br>O Preferring people to procedures<br>O Referring to "we" | O Conforming to previous procedures<br>O Carrying out without challenging<br>O Not questioning the brief<br>O Going your own way<br>O Focusing only on own excellence |
| GUIDANCE | O Looking for added value opportunities<br>O Accepting responsibility for growth and results<br>O Understanding and promoting vision and purpose<br>O Prioritizing high-value opportunities | O Valuing people based only on technical skills<br>O Using only financial indicators<br>O Focusing on people, not results<br>O Going for the easy option<br>O Blaming everyone else for poor performance |

| STATE OF LEADERSHIP | TAKING UP THE NEW | LETTING GO OF THE OLD |
|---|---|---|
| DEVELOPMENT | O Developing talent for the benefit of all<br>O Helping others to perform well<br>O Becoming a mentor<br>O Planning development opportunities<br>O Choosing a team to complement you<br>O Nurturing future leaders | O Prioritizing results above people<br>O Holding on to good people<br>O Failing to delegate enough<br>O Allowing too little time with others<br>O Postponing training if under pressure<br>O Underestimating time for meetings |
| EMBODIMENT | O Facilitating others to grow<br>O Initiating peer networks<br>O Acting as a leader of leaders<br>O Mentoring/coaching leaders | O Focusing only on the organization<br>O Sacrificing social life<br>O Allowing leader-centric power games |

# Coaching for success

**A good coach can accelerate the development of your future leaders, helping them to manage the transitions they need to make to gain leadership experience and develop the suite of competences required to be a top leader within your organization.**

## Releasing potential

It isn't easy to find time to invest in coaching your potential leaders, but there will be a considerable return to you, your team, and the organization if you do. The selection of coaches needs to be undertaken with care—the careers of some of the brightest prospects in your organization will be in their hands.

> Successful **coaching** creates an increased **self-appreciation** in your future leaders of their personal **strengths, competences, approach, and actions**

**Tip**

### COACH VIRTUALLY

Distance is no barrier to effective coaching, but **virtual sessions** do need extra focus to connect and build trust. **Think beyond** scheduled video calls: quick email and text-message check-ins can **give support** at crucial moments, while phone chats—without face-to-face contact—can help people **open up** about difficult information.

## Challenging and supporting

The hallmark of a skilled coach is knowing when to challenge and when to support the individual being coached. Successful coaches work to build self-awareness and release potential, by, for example, unblocking limiting or constricting beliefs or confronting unhelpful behaviors. They encourage the people they are coaching to reflect deeply, think strategically, release their instinctive creativity, and feel good about who they are.

The results of successful coaching should be an increased self-appreciation in your future leaders of their personal strengths, competences, approach, and actions. These newly developed leadership elements, in turn, should align with your organization's stated values and aims.

## The right experience

You may choose to coach your potential leaders yourself, or you may prefer to appoint other internal or external coaches. Whoever you choose, they must have the right business and coaching experience or have received training on how to coach effectively.

Tip

**MAP OUT THE PROCESS**
When providing **coaching,**
**explain** what the process
is, how long it will take,
and what will be covered.
**Encourage** the coachee
to journal their progress.

**Benefiting the business**
Coaching and mentoring—especially of
first-line and middle managers—is often
focused on specific issues or to help
people make leadership transitions.
In this case, experienced mentors from
your organization may be most suitable.
Senior managers may benefit from an
external coach with more experience at
board level. With successful coaching
you may find leaders become better at
innovating and developing the overall
capability of their teams. The effects of
coaching flow through the organization
and provide significant business benefits,
including those listed here:

Retention of key
executives

Enhanced working
relationships

Greater alignment of
individual/corporate
objectives

The benefits
of coaching

New perspectives
on business issues

The effects of coaching
**flow through** the
organization

# Adapting to a changing landscape

**In today's corporate world, the old idea of a job for life has been all but superseded by that of the portfolio career. Leaders now face near-constant transition, and only those who develop the change-management skills to cope will survive. The emphasis has shifted from excelling in a particular corporate position to excelling in one vital project—leading your own life based on consistent principles.**

## Profiting from change

In business today, leaders need to manage and inspire not just their core teams but groups of freelancers, temporary staff, and outsourcers. Engaging such potentially disparate groups to align them with the vision and values of the organization is the new leadership challenge. Leaders today may be heading up a virtual team—with members based globally— formed around a customer problem that needs solving or an innovative idea rather than a group of people physically working together for the same employer. Leaders with the ability to be agile, to build virtual networks, teams, and alliances quickly, will be the long-term winners.

Leaders are looking less and less to their employers to provide a framework or support system for their life—they need to develop it themselves. As an individual aiming to survive in this rapidly changing environment, you must be excellent at understanding customer needs and have supreme confidence in your ability to deliver, and market, yourself. Thinking creatively and with vision, both about your career and personal mission, should become a life-long process and a central theme in your continued success.

**|08**
Identify your next direction for development

**|07**
Refine your brand

**|06**
Practice new skills and behaviors

## Branding yourself

So how do you develop yourself as a leader able to thrive in today's shifting corporate world? One way of answering that is to think of what you can deliver to your customers as a brand. Your brand signals your professional, technical, and functional knowledge and skills, and also your position in the market. Aim to develop yourself much as you would steer a brand. Shape your product (what you offer) to anticipate customer demand, and develop your identity to make the best fit with desirable clients. For example, should your next client be a small enterprise where you can work closely on your entrepreneurial acumen, or should it be a large corporation where you can refresh process management knowledge? Consider your next step carefully—how will it shape your brand?

## How to develop continuously

**01**
Assess your competences and match with customer needs

**02**
Take an assignment to stretch you

**03**
Listen to customers; engage with others; join networks; initiate alliances

**04**
Learn from best practice

**05**
Recognize your potential for development

Leaders with the ability to be **agile,** to build virtual **networks** and alliances quickly, will be the long-term **winners**

# Index

# Acknowledgments

**Stats**

**p.20** "Founder-Led Companies Outperform the Rest—Here's Why", *Harvard Business Review*, March 24, 2016
**p.25** *Leadership & Management in the UK—The Key to Sustainable Growth*, Department for Business, Innovation & Skills, July 2012
**p.32** "Delegating: A Huge Management Challenge for Entrepreneurs", Gallup, April 15, 2015
**p.34** *State of the Workplace Empathy*, Businessolver, 2018
**p.44** *Feedback on Feedback*, Eagle Hill, 2015
**p.47** "3 Ways to Improve Performance Management Conversations", Gartner, December 20, 2019
**p.63** *Succeeding in Disruptive Times: Global Transformation Study*, KPMG, 2016
**p.69** "The Right Culture: Not Just About Employee Satisfaction", Gallup, April 12, 2017
**p.72** *The True Value of Customer Experiences*, Deloitte, 2018
**p.77** "New Survey Reveals 85% of All Jobs Are Filled via Networking", Lou Adler, LinkedIn.com, February 29, 2016
**p.79** "The Productivity Advantage of Serial Entrepreneurs", Kathryn Shaw & Anders Sørensen, *ILR Review*, July 17, 2019
**p.81** "Fostering Creativity at Work: Do Your Managers Push or Crush Innovation?", Gallup, December 19, 2018
**p.85** *Global Human Capital Trends*, Deloitte, 2019
**p.87** "Follow the Leader(ship) Spending", Mike Prokopeak, *Chief Learning Officer*, March 21, 2018

**The publisher would like to thank:**
**Delhi Team**
**DTP Designer:** Jaypal Singh Chauhan, Mrinmoy Mazumdar
**Editor:** Beverly Smart

**Second edition:**
**Senior Art Editor** Gillian Andrews
**Project Editor** Hugo Wilkinson
**Designer** XAB Design
**Editor** Louise Tucker
**UK Editor** Sam Kennedy
**US Editors** Margaret Parrish, Jill Hamilton
**Managing Editor** Stephanie Farrow
**Senior Managing Art Editor** Lee Griffiths
**Production Editor** Nikoleta Parasaki
**Production Controller** Mandy Inness
**Jacket Designer** Mark Cavanagh
**Design Development Manager** Sophia M.T.T.

**Delhi Team:**
**Senior Art Editor** Govind Mittal
**Art Editor** Vikas Chauhan
**DTP Designer** Vishal Bhatia

**First edition:**
**Senior Editor** Peter Jones
**Senior Art Editor** Helen Spencer
**Executive Managing Editor** Adèle Hayward
**Managing Art Editor** Kat Mead
**Art Director** Peter Luff
**Publisher** Stephanie Jackson
**Production Editor** Ben Marcus
**Production Controller** Hema Gohil
**US Editor** Charles Wills

First edition produced for Dorling Kindersley Limited by Cobalt ID, The Stables, Wood Farm, Deopham Road, Attleborough, Norfolk NR17 1AJ
www.cobaltid.co.uk

**Editors**
Louise Abbott, Kati Dye, Maddy King, Marek Walisiewicz